AUTISM ESSENTIALS

A Guide book for understanding and managing Autism

David Greenwood

TABLE OF CONTENTS

+

TABLE OF CONTENTS	1
CHAPTER 1: INTRODUCTION TO AUTISM SPECTRUM DISORDER (ASD)	4
Definition and General Overview	5
Historical Context and Development of the Diagnosis	7
Common Misconceptions and Myths	9
CHAPTER 2: IDENTIFYING SIGNS AND SYMPTOMS OF AUTISM	13
Early Indicators in Infants and Young Children	13
Typical Behavioral Traits	16
Issues Related to Sensory Processing	18
CHAPTER 3: THE DIAGNOSTIC JOURNEY	23
Criteria and Assessments for Diagnosis	24
The Role of Healthcare Professionals	26
The Importance of Early Intervention	28
CHAPTER 4: AUTISM THROUGHOUT LIFE	32
Development in Early Childhood	33
Transitioning into Adolescence	36
Adult Life and Aging with Autism	38
CHAPTER 5: COMMUNICATION AND LANGUAGE SKILLS	42
Delays and Variations in Language Development	43
Using Augmentative and Alternative Communication (AAC)	46
Strategies for Enhancing Communication Skills	49

CHAPTER 6: SOCIAL INTERACTION AND
RELATIONSHIPS   54
    Recognizing and Interpreting Social Cues   55
    Developing and Sustaining Friendships   58
    Navigating Romantic Relationships   61
CHAPTER 7: SENSORY PROCESSING AND
MANAGEMENT   65
    Insights into Sensory Sensitivities   66
    Techniques for Sensory Regulation   69
    Designing Sensory-Friendly Spaces   72
CHAPTER 8: EDUCATIONAL STRATEGIES AND
LEARNING SUPPORT   76
    Crafting Individualized Education Plans (IEPs)   77
    Implementing Classroom Accommodations   80
    Supporting Learning at Home   83
CHAPTER 9: BEHAVIOR MANAGEMENT AND
INTERVENTIONS   88
    Understanding Behavioral Challenges   89
    Positive Behavior Support (PBS) Strategies   92
    Overview of Applied Behavior Analysis (ABA) and Other
    Methods   95
CHAPTER 10: SUPPORTING FAMILIES AND
CAREGIVERS   100
    Managing Family Dynamics   101
    Resources and Support Networks   104
    Prioritizing Self-Care for Caregivers   107
CHAPTER 11: AUTISM AND CO-OCCURRING
CONDITIONS   111
    Common Co-occurring Disorders   112
    Addressing Mental Health Needs   116
    Comprehensive Treatment Approaches   120
CHAPTER 12: EMPLOYMENT READINESS AND
INDEPENDENCE   125
    Preparing for the Workforce   126

Accommodations in the Workplace	129
Encouraging Independence	132
CHAPTER 13: ADVOCACY AND LEGAL RIGHTS	**137**
Understanding Rights and Protections	138
Advocating for Individuals with Autism	141
Promoting Self-Advocacy Skills	143
CHAPTER 14: THE INFLUENCE OF TECHNOLOGY	**148**
Assistive Tools and Technology	149
Online Resources and Support Communities	152
Utilizing Technology for Communication and Education	155
CHAPTER 15: FUTURE DIRECTIONS IN AUTISM RESEARCH	**160**
Current Trends in Research	161
New Therapeutic Innovations	164
The Significance of Inclusive Research	166
CHAPTER 16: FOSTERING A SUPPORTIVE COMMUNITY	**170**
Developing Inclusive Spaces	171
Embracing Neurodiversity	174
How Everyone Can Participate	176
Thank You Message	**180**

CHAPTER 1: INTRODUCTION TO AUTISM SPECTRUM DISORDER (ASD)

"The greatest gift you can give someone is your time, your attention, your love, and your concern." — Joel Osteen

Definition and General Overview

Autism Spectrum Disorder (ASD) is a condition that affects how a person thinks, interacts with others, and behaves. The word "spectrum" means that there are many different ways autism can show itself, with some people having more severe symptoms than others. For example, some individuals may not talk much or may need help with daily tasks, while others may be very intelligent and excel in subjects like math or art.

ASD is usually diagnosed when children are young, but sometimes it isn't noticed until later, especially if the symptoms are mild or if the person has learned ways to cope. Common signs of autism include difficulties making eye contact, trouble understanding social cues, repeating certain actions or phrases, and a strong need for routines. Many people with ASD also experience sensitivities to sensory input, meaning they might be overly sensitive to sounds or textures or not notice them at all.

The effects of autism are different for each person. Some individuals may need a lot of help throughout their lives, while others can manage on their own. It's important to recognize that people with autism can contribute positively to society and often have unique skills and talents.

Historical Context and Development of the Diagnosis

Our understanding of autism has changed a lot over the years. The term "autism" was first used in the early 1900s by a Swiss psychiatrist named Eugen Bleuler to describe someone who was withdrawn from the world. But it wasn't until the 1940s that autism was seen as a separate developmental disorder.

In 1943, Dr. Leo Kanner published a paper that explained the behaviors of children he called "autistic." He noted that these children had trouble interacting socially, communicating, and often displayed repetitive behaviors. Around the same time, an Austrian doctor named Hans Asperger identified another group of children who showed similar but milder symptoms, leading to the diagnosis now known as Asperger's syndrome.

Over the decades, our understanding of autism continued to grow. In 1980, autism was officially included in a medical manual called the Diagnostic and Statistical Manual of Mental Disorders (DSM). In later versions, autism was grouped with other similar conditions under a broader category called pervasive developmental disorders (PDD), which included Asperger's syndrome and PDD-NOS (not otherwise specified).

A major change came in 2013 when the DSM-5 was published. This edition combined different types of autism into one diagnosis called Autism Spectrum Disorder. This change aimed to clarify the different symptoms people with autism may have and to simplify the understanding of the condition.

Common Misconceptions and Myths

Even though more people are learning about Autism Spectrum Disorder, many misunderstandings and myths still exist. One of the biggest myths is that people with autism lack empathy, which means they can't understand or share the feelings of others. While it can be hard for some individuals with autism to read social cues, this doesn't mean they don't feel deeply for others; they may just show their feelings differently.

Another common misconception is that everyone with autism has an intellectual disability. The truth is that autism can be found in people with a wide range of intelligence levels. Some may have difficulties in learning, while others are very bright.

Many believe that autism is caused by bad parenting or a lack of love in early childhood. This idea, known as the "refrigerator mother" theory, has been proven wrong by research that shows autism is actually a complex mix of genetic and environmental factors.

Parents are not to blame for their child having autism.

Some people think that individuals with autism cannot have happy lives or form real friendships. In fact, many people with autism create strong relationships with family, friends, and others in their community. With the right support and understanding, they can succeed in school, work, and personal lives.

Finally, many think autism is a rare condition. In reality, recent studies show that about 1 in 36 children in the United States are diagnosed with ASD. This increase is due to better awareness, more accurate diagnoses, and more people getting the help they need.

In summary, understanding Autism Spectrum Disorder involves looking at its definition, historical background, and the myths surrounding it. As society learns more about autism, it is vital to spread awareness, acceptance, and support for those with ASD. By dispelling myths and promoting understanding, we can help create a world that appreciates the unique qualities of individuals on the autism spectrum.

CHAPTER 2: IDENTIFYING SIGNS AND SYMPTOMS OF AUTISM

"The journey of a thousand miles begins with one step." – Lao Tzu

Early Indicators in Infants and Young Children

Noticing the early signs of Autism Spectrum Disorder (ASD) is important for getting the right help. While every child develops at their own speed, some signs can help parents, caregivers, and professionals recognize children who might be at risk for autism.

Research shows that signs of autism can be seen even in babies. For instance, parents might notice that their infant doesn't respond when they call their name, doesn't make eye contact, or doesn't smile back when someone smiles at them. These signs can be quite subtle and might not be immediately seen as signs of a developmental issue.

By age two, more obvious signs might appear. A child with autism might find it hard to play with others, preferring to play alone. They may not enjoy interactive games like peek-a-boo.

Language development can also be delayed. Some kids may not talk at all, while others might repeat phrases they've heard without really understanding what they mean.

Other signs can include having very specific interests or behaving in unusual ways. For example, a child might focus on spinning the wheels of a toy car for a long time instead of playing with it as most children do. They may also have set routines and get upset if those routines are changed or if they are introduced to new activities.

Typical Behavioral Traits

As children with autism grow older, their unique behaviors may become clearer. Common traits include challenges in social interactions, difficulties in communication, and repetitive or restricted behaviors.

Social interaction can be especially tough for kids with autism. They may have trouble understanding social cues like facial expressions or tone of voice, making it hard to make and keep friends. For example, a child with autism might not notice when a friend is sad and continue playing without acknowledging their feelings. They might also have trouble starting conversations and may talk at others rather than with them, often focusing on topics that interest them alone.

Communication challenges can show up in different ways. Some children with autism might not speak at all, while others may struggle to communicate effectively even if they can talk. They might have a hard time starting conversations or understanding how to take turns in a dialogue. Some may use echolalia, which means they repeat phrases they have heard before, even if it doesn't fit the current conversation.

Repetitive behaviors are also common in autism. These behaviors can include things like hand-flapping, rocking, or spinning. Children may also insist on doing the same activities in the same way repeatedly. For instance, a child might want to take the same route to school every day or eat their meals in a particular order.

The traits of autism can vary greatly from one person to another. Some children may face significant challenges, while others might develop coping strategies and excel in certain skills or areas, often called "splinter skills."

Issues Related to Sensory Processing

Many people with autism have sensory processing issues that can affect their everyday lives. Sensory processing is how the brain understands and reacts to information from our senses—like what we see, hear, smell, taste, and touch. For some individuals with autism, this processing can be different, leading them to be overly sensitive or less sensitive to sensory experiences.

Some kids with autism might be hypersensitive, meaning they can get overwhelmed by sounds or lights that others don't even notice. For example, a child might cover their ears when they hear a vacuum cleaner or feel anxious in busy, noisy places. They might also find certain textures uncomfortable, which can lead to outbursts or wanting to avoid situations that most kids enjoy.

On the other hand, some individuals with autism may be hyposensitive, which means they may not notice sensory input in a typical way. They might not react to pain as other kids do or may seek out intense sensations, like spinning or bumping into things. This can lead to behaviors like wanting to feel physical sensations more intensely or not being aware of dangers in their environment.

Understanding sensory processing issues is key to helping individuals with autism. Creating a sensory-friendly environment can help reduce feelings of being overwhelmed. This can involve using noise-canceling headphones, providing quiet spaces for breaks, or allowing sensory tools like fidget spinners or stress balls to help manage anxiety.

Parents, caregivers, and teachers can also help children with autism navigate sensory experiences. By learning to spot triggers and developing strategies to deal with overwhelming situations, they can help children feel more comfortable in different settings.

In summary, identifying the signs and symptoms of Autism Spectrum Disorder means recognizing early signs in babies and young children, understanding typical behaviors, and being aware of sensory processing issues. Each child with autism is different, and their experiences can vary widely. By learning about these signs and symptoms, parents, teachers, and family members can offer better support and understanding, helping individuals on the autism spectrum thrive and reach their full potential.

CHAPTER 3: THE DIAGNOSTIC JOURNEY

Getting a diagnosis of autism can be a tough and emotional ride for families. It's important to understand what the diagnosis involves, how healthcare professionals help, and why early support matters. Knowing these things can help ensure that people with autism get the support they need to live happy, fulfilling lives.

Criteria and Assessments for Diagnosis

To diagnose Autism Spectrum Disorder (ASD), doctors follow guidelines in a book called the Diagnostic and Statistical Manual of Mental Disorders (DSM-5). According to this book, autism is recognized by difficulties in social communication and behavior patterns that are limited or repetitive. These signs usually show up early in life and can affect how a person functions in school, work, or at home.

When assessing for autism, doctors use different methods, including structured tests and observations. One common tool is called the Autism Diagnostic Observation Schedule (ADOS), where doctors interact with the child to see how they communicate and behave. Another tool is the Autism Diagnostic Interview-Revised (ADI-R), which gathers information from parents about the child's early behaviors and development.

During the evaluation, healthcare professionals will also look at the child's growth milestones and any other conditions they might have, like anxiety or ADHD. Since autism affects everyone differently, with a range of symptoms and severity, the diagnostic process can vary widely from one person to another.

Parents and caregivers are crucial in this journey. They know their child best and can share valuable insights about their behaviors, strengths, and challenges. Keeping a record of social interactions, communication efforts, and any unusual behaviors can be very helpful during assessments.

The Role of Healthcare Professionals

Different healthcare professionals can be involved in diagnosing autism, each with their own expertise. Pediatricians are often the first people parents turn to when they have concerns about their child's development. They can conduct initial screenings and refer families to specialists if they suspect autism or another developmental issue.

Developmental pediatricians specialize in assessing and treating children with developmental delays, including autism. They provide detailed evaluations and can coordinate care among other specialists, like speech therapists, occupational therapists, and psychologists.

Clinical psychologists also play an important role. They assess cognitive skills, social abilities, and emotional health, helping to differentiate autism from other disorders. Sometimes, neurologists are involved to rule out any other brain-related issues that may show similar signs.

It's vital for families to feel comfortable with the professionals involved in the diagnostic journey. Having open conversations with healthcare providers can help ensure that all important information is considered, allowing families to advocate for their child's needs effectively.

The Importance of Early Intervention

A key part of the diagnostic journey is recognizing that early intervention can lead to much better outcomes for individuals with autism. Research shows that children who get the right support early on are more likely to develop important social, communication, and life skills.

Early intervention services are designed to meet each child's unique needs. These may include behavioral therapy, speech and language therapy, occupational therapy, and social skills training. The goal is to help children learn skills that will lead to greater independence and a better quality of life.

One popular method used in early intervention is called Applied Behavior Analysis (ABA). This approach focuses on encouraging positive behaviors and reducing challenging ones through structured teaching. ABA can be personalized for each child and is often done in one-on-one sessions or small groups.

Family support and education are also essential parts of early intervention. Parents and caregivers play a vital role in their child's development, and providing them with resources and training can empower them to effectively support their child's growth. Programs that teach families about autism, helpful communication techniques, and how to create supportive home environments can be incredibly valuable.

Access to early intervention services can differ based on where you live, available resources, and healthcare policies. Many countries have guidelines to make sure children with autism receive timely evaluations and services. Families should actively look for local autism support organizations, community programs, and online resources that offer information and help.

In summary, the diagnostic journey for Autism Spectrum Disorder involves understanding specific criteria, working with various healthcare professionals, and recognizing the importance of early intervention. Although this process can be overwhelming and emotional, it's crucial for families to stay informed and proactive in advocating for their child's needs. By getting a diagnosis and engaging in early intervention services, individuals with autism can receive the support they need to thrive and reach their full potential.

CHAPTER 4: AUTISM THROUGHOUT LIFE

"Life is a journey, not a destination."

Autism is not just something kids have; it's a lifelong journey that changes as people grow up. Understanding how autism affects different stages of life—early childhood, teenage years, and adulthood—can help families, friends, and communities give the right support and guidance to individuals on the autism spectrum. Each stage has its own challenges and chances for growth that can greatly impact a person's happiness and quality of life.

Development in Early Childhood

The early childhood years are really important for kids with Autism Spectrum Disorder (ASD). During this time, children start to learn key skills that will help them in school and when making friends. Spotting signs of autism early can help kids get the help they need to succeed.

Most of the time, signs of autism show up before a child turns three. Some common signs include trouble speaking, difficulty making friends, and sticking to routines or repeating behaviors. For example, a child with autism might avoid eye contact, find it hard to play pretend games, or not show much interest in playing with other kids.

Once a child is diagnosed, getting early help is super important. This help might include different therapies like behavior therapy, speech therapy, and occupational therapy that are designed just for them. One of the most helpful approaches is called Applied Behavior Analysis (ABA), which focuses on teaching positive behaviors and important skills in a structured way.

Parents and caregivers play a big role in helping their children grow. They can encourage learning by doing activities together that promote social skills and communication. For instance, reading stories together, playing games that involve taking turns, and setting up routines can help kids learn. Community programs that offer playgroups or support for families can also be great resources.

It's also important to understand how a child feels about their senses. Many kids with autism might be very sensitive to things like loud noises, certain textures, or bright lights. Making the home a comfortable place for them can help them feel safe and happy.

Transitioning into Adolescence

As children with autism reach their teenage years, they face new challenges and changes. This time is filled with big physical, emotional, and social developments, which can be particularly complicated for them.

Teenagers with autism may feel more anxious because of social pressures and changes in their bodies. Many have a hard time understanding and expressing their feelings, which can lead to feelings of loneliness and frustration. This is a time when friendships become very important, and the desire to fit in with peers grows stronger. Because of this, some teenagers may avoid social situations or face bullying, so it's essential for parents and teachers to create a supportive environment.

Education becomes very important during these years, as schools can help prepare teens for life as adults. Individualized Education Programs (IEPs) should be updated to match the teen's needs, focusing on life skills, job training, and social skills. Joining clubs or sports can also help teens make friends and build confidence.

Teaching life skills is especially important for teenagers. Learning things like cooking, personal care, and budgeting can help them become more independent. Social skills training can also help them handle tricky social situations and make lasting friendships.

Support groups for teens and their families can be great places to share experiences and support one another. Connecting with others who face similar challenges can help create a sense of belonging.

Adult Life and Aging with Autism

The path of autism doesn't stop after teenage years; it continues into adulthood. Many adults with autism lead fulfilling lives, but they still face challenges. It's important to understand what adults with autism need to create supportive environments that encourage independence and happiness.

For many adults on the spectrum, finding a job is a big priority. They often have unique skills that can be valuable in the workplace. However, finding and keeping a job can be tough because of difficulties with social interactions and sensory sensitivities. Programs that offer job training and support can help adults gain the skills and confidence they need to succeed in the workforce.

Social relationships remain crucial in adulthood. While some adults with autism build meaningful friendships, others may feel lonely. Encouraging participation in social activities, support groups, or hobby clubs can provide chances to connect and make friends.

As individuals with autism get older, they may face more health and wellness challenges. It's vital to recognize the importance of mental health support and access to healthcare. Regular check-ups, therapy, and community resources can help adults manage the complexities of life while dealing with any mental health concerns.

For older adults on the spectrum, planning for the future is very important. Topics like housing, finances, and healthcare become more significant. Families should have conversations about future planning to make sure their loved ones have the support and resources they need as they age.

In conclusion, the journey of autism lasts a lifetime, covering many stages from early childhood to adulthood and beyond. Each phase brings its own challenges and opportunities for growth. By understanding these stages and providing the right support, families, friends, and communities can help individuals with autism thrive and lead fulfilling lives. Embracing the unique strengths and qualities of each person on the spectrum is essential for creating a more inclusive and understanding society.

CHAPTER 5: COMMUNICATION AND LANGUAGE SKILLS

"Words are the voice of the heart." - Confucius

Effective communication is a vital part of how we interact with one another and form connections. For people with Autism Spectrum Disorder (ASD), communication can be quite different from what is usual. Recognizing these differences and finding ways to support communication development is essential for helping those with autism make meaningful connections and improve their lives. In this chapter, we will look at the common challenges in language development, how augmentative and alternative communication (AAC) can help, and various strategies to enhance communication skills.

Delays and Variations in Language Development

Language development for children with autism often doesn't follow the same path as it does for their peers. Some kids with autism might have a rich vocabulary and engage in conversations, while others might struggle significantly with their

These variations in language development can create barriers to effective communication and social interaction. That's why it's important for caregivers and teachers to recognize each person's unique way of communicating. Identifying these differences early and providing support can significantly help children with autism navigate social situations and express themselves better.

Using Augmentative and Alternative Communication (AAC)

For individuals with autism who find it hard to communicate verbally, augmentative and alternative communication (AAC) can be a helpful tool. AAC includes different methods and tools to help people express their thoughts, needs, and feelings. There are two main types of AAC: aided and unaided communication.

1. Unaided Communication: This includes ways of communicating that don't need any extra tools, like gestures, facial expressions, body language, or sign language. Teaching these methods can help individuals communicate without words.

2. Aided Communication: This involves using tools or devices to help with communication. Examples include picture boards and communication apps that allow people to select images or symbols to express what they want to

say. These tools can help them communicate in different situations.

Using AAC can significantly improve how individuals with autism communicate. It can lessen the frustration of not being understood, help them interact with others more, and enhance their overall quality of life. Caregivers, teachers, and speech-language therapists can work together to find the right AAC methods for each person, adapting the approach to fit their specific communication needs.

Strategies for Enhancing Communication Skills

Improving communication skills for individuals with autism requires a well-rounded approach that considers their unique strengths and challenges. Here are some effective strategies to help enhance communication:

1. Modeling Language: Caregivers and teachers can demonstrate how to use language effectively by speaking clearly and using simple sentences. Describing what they are doing as it happens and using visual aids can encourage individuals to respond and practice their language skills.

2. Visual Supports: Many individuals with autism learn best through visuals. Picture schedules, visual cues, and social stories can help them understand routines and social situations. These supports can also assist in learning new vocabulary.

3. Encouraging Social Interaction: Providing opportunities for socializing with peers can improve communication skills. Group activities, playdates, and social skills training can help individuals practice communicating in real-life situations. Positive reinforcement can build their confidence to engage with others.

4. Promoting Choice-Making: Allowing individuals to make choices can boost their communication skills and give them a sense of empowerment. Providing options for activities or snacks can encourage them to express their preferences, whether verbally or using AAC tools.

5. Using Technology: Technology can play a big role in supporting communication skills. Various apps and software are designed to help individuals with autism develop their language skills and use AAC effectively. These tools can make learning enjoyable and offer chances for practice.

6. Establishing Routines: Consistent routines can help individuals with autism feel more secure and reduce anxiety. Setting up a daily schedule allows for structured opportunities to practice communication. When they know what to expect, they may feel more comfortable communicating during specific activities.

In summary, communication and language skills are vital for individuals with autism to connect with others and understand their environment. While there are challenges in language development, recognizing these differences is crucial for providing effective support. Augmentative and alternative communication (AAC) serves as a valuable tool to improve communication. By using strategies to enhance communication skills, caregivers and educators can create an environment that encourages meaningful interactions. Ultimately, helping individuals with autism express themselves will lead to greater understanding, connection, and fulfillment in their lives.

CHAPTER 6: SOCIAL INTERACTION AND RELATIONSHIPS

"The greatest gift of life is friendship, and I have received it." -Hubert H. Humphrey

Social interaction is a key part of life, helping us build friendships and feel happy. However, for people with Autism Spectrum Disorder (ASD), making friends and connecting with others can be challenging. In this chapter, we will learn about recognizing social cues, making and keeping friendships, and navigating romantic relationships in a way that is easy to understand.

Recognizing and Interpreting Social Cues

One major challenge for individuals with autism is understanding social cues. These cues are the small signals we use to communicate feelings, thoughts, and intentions without using words. They include things like body language, facial expressions, tone of voice, and unwritten social rules. Here are some areas where people with autism might need extra help:

1. Understanding Nonverbal Communication: A lot of

communication happens without words. For example, a smile usually means someone is friendly, while a frown can mean they are upset. People with autism may have trouble recognizing these signals. Teaching them to understand common facial expressions and body language can help them see how others are feeling.

2. Reading the Room: It's important to know when to talk, listen, or join a conversation based on how others are acting. Individuals with autism may find it hard to tell if others are bored or excited. Practicing social scenarios through role-playing can help them learn when to speak and how to respond.

3. Understanding Context: The meaning of what someone says can change depending on the situation. A joke might be funny in one place but not in another. Parents, teachers, and caregivers can help individuals understand different social situations and what responses are appropriate for each.

4. Practice and Reinforcement: Recognizing social cues gets easier with practice. Encouraging individuals to take part in social events, giving feedback, and praising positive interactions can help them build confidence. Visual aids and social stories can also support their learning.

Developing and Sustaining Friendships

Friendships are important because they offer support and companionship. However, making and keeping friends can be tricky for people with autism. Here are some ways to help:

1. Encouraging Shared Interests: Finding things in common is often the basis of friendships. Individuals with autism might have unique interests that can help them connect with others. Encouraging participation in activities related to their interests, like clubs or classes, can help them meet peers who enjoy the same things.

2. Social Skills Training: Teaching specific social skills can help individuals navigate friendships better. Social skills training can cover things like how to start a conversation, listen carefully, and know when to change the topic. Practicing these skills in fun activities or role-playing can make learning easier.

3. Fostering Empathy: Empathy is the ability to understand and share the feelings of others. Talking about emotions and feelings can help individuals with autism relate better to their friends. Working on team projects or problem-solving together can also build empathy and strengthen friendships.

4. Encouraging Communication: Good communication is crucial for friendships. Encouraging individuals to share their thoughts and feelings openly can help build trust with their friends. Teaching them how to ask questions, give compliments, and show support can create stronger connections.

5. Maintaining Friendships: Friendships need effort to stay strong. Encouraging individuals to regularly reach out to their friends—whether by texting, using social media, or meeting up—can help keep those connections alive. Small gestures, like remembering birthdays or sharing experiences, can also maintain friendships.

Navigating Romantic Relationships

Romantic relationships are an important part of growing up, but they can be particularly challenging for people with autism. Here are some tips for supporting individuals in romantic relationships:

1. Discussing Relationships: Having open conversations about what relationships are can help individuals understand dating better. Talking about what makes a healthy relationship, such as respect and communication, can clear up confusion. Discussing feelings related to attraction can also help them understand their own experiences.

2. Practicing Social Skills in Dating Contexts: Just like friendships, practicing social skills related to dating is important. This can include learning how to start a conversation with someone they like, how to ask someone out, and how to read social cues during a date. Role-playing these situations can help them practice in a safe space.

3. Understanding Boundaries: Discussing personal boundaries is crucial in romantic relationships. Individuals with autism may need explicit guidance on how to set boundaries and understand their partner's boundaries. Talking about consent, personal space, and emotional

boundaries can help them navigate dating better.

4. Managing Rejection: Rejection is a part of dating, and it can be tough for anyone, especially for people with autism. Teaching them how to cope with disappointment and move forward can help them deal with setbacks. Encourage them to see rejection as a normal part of life instead of a personal failure.

5. Using Technology Wisely: Technology, like dating apps and social media, can help individuals meet potential partners. Teaching them how to use these platforms responsibly, including being aware of online

etiquette and privacy, is important. Encourage them to take their time and feel comfortable with the pace of the relationship.

In summary, social interaction and relationships are vital to our lives, but they can be difficult for people with autism. By learning to recognize social cues, develop friendships, and navigate romantic relationships, individuals with autism can improve their social skills and build meaningful connections. With the right support and practice, they can enjoy more fulfilling relationships and experiences in their lives.

CHAPTER 7: SENSORY PROCESSING AND MANAGEMENT

"The senses are the gateway to understanding the world."

Sensory processing is how our brains take in and understand information from the world around us using our senses, like sight, sound, and touch. For individuals with Autism Spectrum Disorder (ASD), this processing can be very different from what most people experience. Many people with autism may have unique reactions to sensory input, which can either be too much or too little. In this chapter, we will look at sensory sensitivities, ways to help manage these sensitivities, and how to create spaces that are comfortable for individuals with autism.

Insights into Sensory Sensitivities

Understanding sensory sensitivities is key to recognizing how they affect the daily lives of individuals with autism. Sensory sensitivities can appear in different ways, affecting one or more of our senses. Here are some important points about these sensitivities:

1. Heightened Sensitivity: Many people with autism may be more sensitive to

sensory input. For example, common sounds like buzzing lights or noise in a crowded place can feel overwhelming. This extra sensitivity can lead to discomfort, anxiety, or meltdowns. What seems like a small sound to someone else can be very distracting or distressing for someone with autism.

2. Diminished Sensitivity: On the other hand, some individuals may not react strongly to sensory stimuli. They might not notice pain like others do or may be less aware of temperature changes. This reduced sensitivity can be risky, as they might not realize they are hurt or too hot or cold. Understanding these differences helps caregivers and teachers respond better.

3. Sensory Overload and Shutdowns: When there's too much sensory input, individuals with autism may feel sensory overload. This can lead to feelings of anxiety or even meltdowns. Some people may respond to this overload by shutting down, withdrawing from their surroundings, and becoming unresponsive. It's important to recognize signs of overload so caregivers can help in time.
4. Individual Variation: Everyone with autism is different and has their own sensory profile. Some may be sensitive to specific sounds, while others may be more affected by what they see. Observing each person's sensory likes and dislikes is crucial for providing good support.

Techniques for Sensory Regulation

Using different techniques can help individuals with autism manage their sensory experiences and find a balance. Here are some helpful strategies:

1. Sensory Breaks: Giving individuals time away from busy places for sensory breaks can help them deal with overwhelming input. These breaks can involve stepping back from loud environments or using calming tools like fidget toys. Regular breaks can prevent overload and help them self-regulate.

2. Deep Pressure Activities: Many individuals with autism find deep pressure calming. Activities that provide firm pressure, like squeezing a stress ball or using a weighted blanket, can help them feel more secure. These activities help them feel grounded and relaxed.

3. Sensory Diets: A sensory diet is a customized plan that includes specific activities to help individuals manage their sensory needs. This plan can include a mix of calming and alerting activities tailored to the person's needs. Working with occupational therapists can help create effective sensory diets.

4. Mindfulness and Relaxation Techniques: Teaching techniques like deep breathing, yoga, or guided imagery can help individuals manage anxiety and sensory overload. These practices encourage self-awareness and help individuals learn how to calm themselves when things feel overwhelming.

5. Use of Visual Supports: Visual tools, like schedules or social stories, can help individuals understand when to take sensory breaks and what activities they can do to manage their sensory experiences. These supports can provide structure and lessen anxiety related to sensory overload.

Designing Sensory-Friendly Spaces

Creating spaces that are friendly for sensory needs is vital for supporting individuals with autism in managing their experiences. Here are some tips for designing these spaces:

1. Quiet Zones: Adding quiet zones or sensory rooms in schools, workplaces, and public places can give individuals a safe space when sensory input becomes too much. These areas should have calming items like soft lighting, comfortable seating, noise-canceling headphones, and sensory tools like weighted blankets.

2. Adjustable Lighting: Lighting can greatly impact how someone feels. Bright, fluorescent lights can be too much for many individuals with autism. Using adjustable lighting, like dimmable lights or soft natural light, can create a more comfortable atmosphere. Choosing soft colors and avoiding harsh contrasts can also help.

3. Sound Management: Soundproofing rooms or using materials that absorb sound can help reduce background noise. Offering options to listen to calming music or white noise can create a more pleasant auditory environment. It's essential to consider noise levels in shared spaces and find ways to reduce distractions.

4. Flexible Spaces: Creating adaptable spaces that can change for different activities can meet various sensory needs. For example, areas that can be rearranged for group activities or quiet time allow individuals to choose how they want to interact with their environment. Adding sensory-friendly furniture, like bean bags or soft mats, can make spaces more inviting.

5. Natural Elements: Including natural elements, like plants or water features, can positively impact sensory experiences. Nature tends to have a calming effect and can help individuals feel more grounded. Providing opportunities for outdoor activities and

exploration can further support sensory regulation.

In summary, understanding sensory processing and sensitivities is essential for helping individuals with autism. By recognizing their unique sensory experiences, using effective regulation techniques, and designing sensory-friendly spaces, caregivers and educators can create environments that promote comfort, reduce anxiety, and enhance well-being. Supporting sensory needs is crucial for fostering independence and helping individuals with autism thrive in their daily lives.

CHAPTER 8: EDUCATIONAL STRATEGIES AND LEARNING SUPPORT

"Education is the most powerful weapon which you can use to change the world." – Nelson Mandela

Education is an important part of life for everyone, including those with Autism Spectrum Disorder (ASD). It's essential to know how to help students with autism succeed in school. This chapter will discuss how to create Individualized Education Plans (IEPs), make classroom adjustments, and support learning at home.

Crafting Individualized Education Plans (IEPs)

An Individualized Education Plan (IEP) is a legal document that describes what a student with a disability needs to succeed in school. It is specifically designed to help students with autism. Here's how to create an effective IEP:

1. Teamwork Matters: Creating an IEP involves a team of people, such as the student's parents, teachers, school psychologists, and other professionals. Working together is important to make

sure the IEP reflects the student's unique strengths and challenges.

2. Understanding Needs: Before making an IEP, it's necessary to assess the student's academic skills, social abilities, sensory preferences, and other areas of concern. This can include tests, observations, and input from parents and teachers. The more information gathered, the better the IEP will be.

3. Setting Clear Goals: A good IEP should include specific goals that are measurable and realistic for the student. These goals can cover both academic and non-academic areas, like social skills and behavior. For instance, an academic goal could be for the student

to improve their reading skills, while a social goal could involve practicing taking turns in group activities.

4. Defining Services and Supports: The IEP should clearly list the services and support the student will receive to achieve their goals. This may include special education services, speech therapy, or counseling, and it should specify how often these services will be provided and by whom.

5. Regular Review and Adjustments: An IEP isn't just made once; it should be reviewed and updated regularly, at least once a year. During these reviews, the team checks the student's progress and makes changes if necessary. This keeps the IEP effective as the student grows and develops.

Implementing Classroom Accommodations

Classroom accommodations help students with autism access their learning materials and participate in class. Here are some strategies for making accommodations in the classroom:

1. Creating a Sensory-Friendly Environment: Make the classroom a comfortable space by reducing distractions. This can involve using soft lighting, lowering noise levels, providing noise-canceling headphones, and allowing the use of fidget tools. Having quiet areas for breaks can also be helpful.

2. Using Visual Supports: Many students with autism benefit from visual tools, such as picture schedules, visual timers, and charts that outline daily routines. These aids help students know what to expect, reducing anxiety and making it easier for them to focus.

3. Establishing Structured Routines: A consistent daily routine helps students with autism feel secure and lowers anxiety. Use visual schedules to outline the day's activities and communicate any changes clearly and ahead of time.

4. Flexible Teaching Methods: Since every student learns differently, incorporating various teaching styles—like hands-on activities, visual aids, and

group work—can help meet the diverse needs of students with autism. Allowing students to show their understanding in different ways, such as through presentations or creative projects, can enhance engagement.

5. Encouraging Peer Support and Social Interaction: Positive peer interactions are important for students with autism. Assigning a buddy for group work can help them navigate social situations. Additionally, explicitly teaching social skills through role-playing and structured activities can improve their ability to interact with classmates.

5. Frequent Check-Ins: Teachers should regularly check in with students

to see how they are understanding the material and to gauge their emotional well-being. This helps identify struggles early and builds a supportive relationship between the teacher and the student.

Supporting Learning at Home

Learning continues at home, and supporting it is crucial for reinforcing what students learn at school. Here are some ways parents and caregivers can support students with autism in their learning:

1. Creating a Structured Home Environment: Just like in the

classroom, having a consistent routine at home helps students feel secure and ready to learn. Create a daily schedule that includes time for homework, chores, play, and breaks.

2. Engaging in Educational Activities: Incorporate learning into everyday life. This can include cooking together (measuring ingredients reinforces math skills), reading, playing educational games, or visiting educational places like museums. Making learning part of daily life helps keep it fun and interesting.

3. Encouraging Communication Skills: Promote open communication by giving the student chances to express their thoughts and feelings. Engage in conversations, ask open-ended

questions, and model good communication. This can improve their speaking and listening skills.

4. Being Consistent with Expectations: Consistency helps reinforce behavior and rules at home. Use clear, simple language to explain what is expected. Having consistent consequences for behavior, both good and bad, helps students understand what is expected and develop self-control.

5. Collaborating with Teachers: Keep in touch with teachers to stay updated on the student's progress and any areas where they may need help. Sharing what works at home can help teachers support the student better in school.

6. Celebrating Achievements: Recognize and celebrate the student's achievements, no matter how small. Positive reinforcement boosts their confidence and motivates them to keep trying. Creating a reward system for reaching goals can make learning more enjoyable.

In conclusion, helping individuals with autism in their educational journey requires teamwork. By creating individualized education plans, making classroom adjustments, and supporting learning at home, parents, teachers, and support staff can help students with autism reach their full potential. With the right strategies and support, individuals with autism can navigate their educational experiences successfully and build a strong foundation for lifelong learning.

CHAPTER 9: BEHAVIOR MANAGEMENT AND INTERVENTIONS

"The greatest way to make a difference is to believe in someone."

Behavior management is a key part of helping people with Autism Spectrum Disorder (ASD). By understanding the behavioral challenges they face and using effective strategies, we can help improve their lives. In this chapter, we'll explore the reasons behind these behaviors, discuss Positive Behavior

Support (PBS) strategies, and look at Applied Behavior Analysis (ABA) along with other methods.

Understanding Behavioral Challenges

Individuals with autism may exhibit different behavioral challenges, such as meltdowns, aggression, self-injury, or withdrawal. These behaviors often have a purpose, like expressing unmet needs, showing frustration, or reacting to overwhelming situations. To help effectively, we need to understand why these behaviors occur.

1. Communication Difficulties: Many individuals with autism find it hard to

express their thoughts and feelings verbally. When they struggle to communicate, they might show their feelings through different behaviors, which can lead to frustration and more challenging actions.

2. Sensory Sensitivities: People with autism can be more sensitive to sounds, lights, or textures. This heightened sensitivity can make them uncomfortable or distressed, causing them to react in certain ways to escape or cope with overwhelming sensations.

3. Routine and Predictability: Many individuals with autism feel more comfortable when things are predictable and follow a routine.

Changes in their environment or schedule can lead to anxiety and behavioral issues. For example, if a routine is disrupted, a meltdown may happen.

4. Emotional Regulation: Managing emotions can be difficult for individuals with autism. When they feel overwhelmed, anxious, or frustrated, they may have outbursts because they can't control their emotions.

5. Coping Mechanisms: Some challenging behaviors may actually be coping strategies. For instance, a child might engage in repetitive movements or sounds (often called stimming) to calm themselves when feeling stressed.

Positive Behavior Support (PBS) Strategies

Positive Behavior Support (PBS) is an approach that focuses on improving the lives of individuals with autism by encouraging positive behaviors and reducing challenging ones. PBS is about understanding why behaviors happen and providing the right support. Here are some key strategies:

1. Identify Triggers: To effectively use PBS, we first need to identify what causes the challenging behaviors. Observing the individual in different situations can help us understand what triggers their behavior.

2. Teach Alternative Behaviors: After figuring out the triggers, we can teach the individual better ways to express themselves. For example, if a child screams to get something, we can teach them to use pictures or signs to communicate their needs instead.

3. Reinforce Positive Behavior: It's essential to reward good behavior. This can be done through praise, small rewards, or extra privileges when the person shows positive actions.

4. Create Structured Environments: Having a clear and structured environment can help reduce anxiety and behavioral challenges. Using visual schedules, timers, and consistent

routines can help individuals with autism feel more secure.

5. Teach Coping Skills: Helping individuals learn coping strategies can improve their ability to manage stress and emotions. Techniques like deep breathing, counting, or using stress-relief tools (like stress balls) can assist them in controlling their feelings.

6. Involve the Individual: When possible, it's helpful to involve the individual in discussions about their behavior and what strategies can help them. This gives them a sense of control and encourages them to engage in positive behaviors.

Overview of Applied Behavior Analysis (ABA) and Other Methods

Applied Behavior Analysis (ABA) is one of the most recognized and studied interventions for individuals with autism. It uses specific behavioral principles to increase good behaviors and decrease challenging ones. Here's a summary of ABA and other methods:

1. What is ABA? ABA is based on the idea that behavior is influenced by the environment. It involves breaking down complex skills into smaller steps and reinforcing each step as the individual learns.

2. Data Collection: ABA practitioners track data about behaviors to see progress and make decisions about what strategies are working. This helps identify trends and allows for adjustments to be made.

3. Functional Behavior Assessment (FBA): A key part of ABA is conducting a Functional Behavior Assessment, which helps figure out why certain behaviors happen. Understanding the reasons allows practitioners to create effective support plans.

4. Individualized Approach: ABA is tailored to meet the unique needs of each person. Goals are set based on the individual's strengths, interests, and

challenges to ensure the intervention is relevant and engaging.

5. Other Behavioral Methods: In addition to ABA, there are other methods that can help, such as:

Cognitive Behavioral Therapy (CBT): This helps individuals recognize and change negative thoughts and behaviors. While it's usually better for older children and adults, it can be adapted for younger individuals with autism.

Social Skills Training: This focuses on teaching social skills through structured activities like role-playing and social stories, helping individuals improve their communication and interaction skills.

Natural Environment Teaching (NET): NET teaches skills in everyday settings rather than just structured environments. This method emphasizes learning through play and real-life situations.

6. Collaboration with Families: Working with families is essential for successful behavior management. Involving parents and caregivers in the process helps reinforce strategies at home and school, providing more consistent support.

Understanding and managing behavioral challenges in individuals with autism is vital for their growth and well-being. By recognizing the causes of behaviors, using Positive Behavior Support strategies, and applying evidence-based methods like ABA, caregivers and educators can create supportive environments that encourage positive behaviors. With the right interventions in place, individuals with autism can learn, develop, and thrive in their daily lives.

CHAPTER 10: SUPPORTING FAMILIES AND CAREGIVERS

"Alone, we can do so little; together, we can do so much." – Helen Keller

Supporting individuals with Autism Spectrum Disorder (ASD) means looking after not just the person with autism but also their whole family and caregivers. Families and caregivers face many challenges as they deal with autism, which can affect their relationships, emotions, and overall happiness. In this chapter, we will talk about how to manage family relationships, find helpful resources and support, and the importance of taking care of caregivers themselves.

Managing Family Dynamics

When autism is part of a family, it can change how family members relate to each other and their responsibilities. Understanding and managing these changes is important for creating a supportive home. Here are some key ideas:

1. Communication is Key: It's important for family members to talk openly about their feelings, worries, and needs. Having regular family

meetings can help everyone share their thoughts and work together to solve problems.

2. Involvement of Siblings: Brothers and sisters of kids with autism might feel proud, but they can also feel jealous or ignored. Involving siblings in conversations about autism can help them understand their brother or sister better. Doing fun activities together can help siblings bond and become closer.

3. Defining Roles and Responsibilities: Autism can change the roles family members play at home. It's important to talk openly about who does what so everyone knows their responsibilities. Parents should consider each other's

strengths and their child's needs to make sure everyone feels important and included.

4. Managing Stress and Conflict: Caring for someone with autism can be stressful, and this stress can lead to conflicts within the family. Learning conflict resolution skills and getting help from professionals, like therapists, can help families get through tough times together.

5. Celebrating Achievements: It's important to celebrate the achievements of the person with autism, no matter how small. Family members should take time to acknowledge progress,

which helps everyone feel united and happy.

Resources and Support Networks

Families caring for individuals with autism can benefit greatly from various resources and support networks. Here are some useful options:

1. Local and National Autism Organizations: Organizations like the Autism Society and Autism Speaks offer resources, support groups, and educational materials for families. Many have local branches to connect families with nearby support.

2. Parent Support Groups: Meeting other parents of kids with autism can provide a sense of community and understanding. These groups allow parents to share experiences and advice with each other.

3. Professional Support Services: Families can benefit from professional services such as therapists and counselors who specialize in autism. These experts can give personalized support and guidance to help manage specific issues.

4. Educational Resources: Many families look for information about educational options for their children with autism. Researching local schools

and special education programs can help families make informed choices.

5. Financial Assistance Programs: Caring for a child with autism can be expensive. Families should look into financial aid, grants, and insurance options that can help cover the costs of therapies and medical care.

6. Community Activities: Many communities have programs and events for individuals with autism and their families. Joining these activities can help families feel connected and supported.

Prioritizing Self-Care for Caregivers

Caregiving can be very demanding, and caregivers often forget to take care of their own needs. Here are some important self-care strategies for caregivers:

1. Recognize the Importance of Self-Care: Caregivers need to understand that taking care of themselves is essential, not selfish. When they prioritize their own health, they can provide better support to their loved ones.

2. Establish a Routine: Creating a daily routine that includes time for self-care

can help caregivers find balance. This might mean taking a few minutes for meditation, exercise, or simply relaxing.

3. Seek Support: Caregivers should not hesitate to ask for help. Whether it's from family, friends, or professionals, sharing responsibilities can provide relief and allow caregivers to recharge.

4. Engage in Hobbies and Interests: Caregivers should make time for activities they enjoy, like reading or gardening. Doing things they love can reduce stress and improve mental health.

5. Practice Mindfulness and Relaxation Techniques: Mindfulness and relaxation exercises can help caregivers manage stress. Even a few minutes of mindfulness can make a big difference in how caregivers feel.

6. Connect with Other Caregivers: Joining support groups or online forums for caregivers can create a sense of community. Sharing experiences with others can help caregivers feel less alone.

Supporting families and caregivers of individuals with autism is crucial for creating a positive and nurturing environment. By managing family relationships, using available resources and support networks, and prioritizing self-care, families can improve their well-being and provide the best support for their loved ones. When caregivers take care of themselves and work together as a family, they help individuals with autism thrive and succeed.

CHAPTER 11: AUTISM AND CO-OCCURRING CONDITIONS

"Understanding others is the beginning of wisdom."

Autism Spectrum Disorder (ASD) is a complex condition that affects how people communicate, behave, and interact with others. A key part of understanding autism is knowing that many people with ASD also have other health issues that can make life more challenging. These additional conditions can complicate how we diagnose and treat autism, so it's important to take a complete look at each individual to help them succeed. In this chapter, we will explore common co-occurring disorders, how to address mental health needs, and the best treatment approaches.

Common Co-occurring Disorders

Co-occurring disorders are health issues that can happen along with autism. While not everyone with autism will have these additional conditions, many do. Understanding these connections is essential for providing effective support. Here are some of the most common co-occurring conditions:

1. Attention-Deficit/Hyperactivity Disorder (ADHD): Many people with autism also have ADHD. This condition makes it hard to pay attention and can cause hyperactivity and impulsiveness. These symptoms can look similar to behaviors seen in autism, making it important to understand the differences for proper treatment.

2. Anxiety Disorders: Anxiety is very common among individuals with autism. Studies show that about 40% of people with autism experience significant anxiety symptoms, such as general worries, fear of social situations, or specific phobias. Anxiety can make it harder to interact with others and manage everyday life.

3. Depression: People with autism are more likely to experience depression, especially during their teenage years and as adults. Feelings of loneliness, trouble with friendships, and challenges with self-identity can lead to depressive symptoms.

4. Obsessive-Compulsive Disorder (OCD): OCD involves having unwanted thoughts (obsessions) and repeating certain actions (compulsions). Some individuals with autism may show repetitive behaviors or strong interests, which can sometimes overlap with OCD symptoms.

5. Learning Disabilities: Learning disabilities, like dyslexia or dyscalculia, are also common among individuals with autism. These conditions can impact how someone learns and may require special educational strategies.

6. Sleep Disorders: Many people with autism have trouble sleeping, whether it's falling asleep, staying asleep, or getting good-quality rest. Sleep problems can greatly affect how someone feels and functions during the day.

Recognizing and understanding these co-occurring conditions is vital for families, teachers, and healthcare providers. Each condition needs specific strategies and help tailored to the individual's needs.

Addressing Mental Health Needs

Mental health is a critical part of overall well-being, and this is true for individuals with autism as well. To help people with autism and their co-occurring conditions, we can use several key strategies:

1. Early Identification and Assessment: Finding co-occurring conditions early is essential for effective help. Regular check-ups for anxiety, depression, ADHD, and other mental health issues should be done to catch any problems as they come up. This proactive

approach allows for timely support and treatment.

2. Collaborative Care Models: Taking care of mental health for individuals with autism should involve many professionals working together. This includes psychologists, psychiatrists, social workers, and occupational therapists. When everyone collaborates, it ensures that all parts of a person's health are considered in their treatment.

3. Individualized Treatment Plans: Treatment should be customized to meet each person's specific needs, considering both autism and any additional conditions. This may include a mix of behavioral therapies,

medications, and strategies to help them cope. Treatment plans should be flexible and updated as the person's needs change.

4. Creating a Supportive Environment: Families and caregivers play an essential role in mental health support. Creating a space that encourages open communication, understanding, and acceptance can greatly affect someone's emotional well-being. Healthy routines, social activities, and self-expression help individuals feel safe and valued.

5. Teaching Coping Skills: Teaching individuals with autism coping strategies to manage anxiety and stress

is important. This can include relaxation methods, mindfulness techniques, and social skills training. Learning these skills helps individuals handle challenges better and improves their overall quality of life.

6. Promoting Social Connections: Encouraging social interactions can help reduce feelings of isolation and loneliness. Taking part in community events, support groups, or social skills programs offers valuable opportunities for individuals with autism to meet others and form meaningful relationships.

Comprehensive Treatment Approaches

To effectively support individuals with autism and co-occurring conditions, a comprehensive treatment approach is essential. This means using various strategies and methods to address the full range of a person's needs:

1. Behavioral Interventions: Approaches like Applied Behavior Analysis (ABA) and other behavioral therapies can help with specific challenges related to autism and co-occurring conditions. These therapies focus on promoting positive behaviors and reducing difficult ones through structured techniques.

2. Medication Management: Sometimes, medication is needed to help manage symptoms of co-occurring conditions like anxiety, depression, or ADHD. A qualified healthcare provider can evaluate the individual's needs and prescribe appropriate medications while considering how they might interact with autism-related behaviors.

3. Therapeutic Support: Psychotherapy, including cognitive-behavioral therapy (CBT), can be effective in helping individuals with autism and their co-occurring mental health conditions. Therapy can provide a safe space for individuals to explore their feelings, develop coping strategies, and work through challenges.

4. Occupational and Speech Therapy: These therapies can address specific developmental and communication challenges associated with autism and co-occurring conditions. Occupational therapy can help individuals learn daily living skills, while speech therapy can improve communication abilities.

5. Family Involvement: Involving families in the treatment process is crucial. Family therapy can help address dynamics that may affect the individual's mental health and overall well-being. Educating families about autism and co-occurring conditions fosters understanding and support.

6. Regular Monitoring and Evaluation: Regularly checking a person's progress is important to ensure that treatment strategies are working. Frequent evaluations can help identify any new issues and allow for adjustments to the treatment plan as needed.

Understanding how autism relates to co-occurring conditions is essential for providing complete support. By recognizing common co-occurring disorders, addressing mental health needs, and using holistic treatment approaches, families, caregivers, and professionals can work together to improve the quality of life for individuals with autism. A collaborative and proactive approach ensures that individuals receive the necessary support to thrive, both emotionally and socially.

CHAPTER 12: EMPLOYMENT READINESS AND INDEPENDENCE

"Success is not the key to happiness. Happiness is the key to success. If you love what you are doing, you will be successful." – Albert Schweitzer

Finding a good job is an important goal for many people, including those with autism. Having a job helps people become more independent, meet new friends, feel better about themselves, and improve their overall quality of life. In this chapter, we will talk about how to get ready for work, what support people with autism might need at their jobs, and how to help them become more independent as they grow up.

Preparing for the Workforce

Getting ready for a job starts long before someone actually applies for one. It involves learning important skills, gaining experience, and building confidence. Here are some key areas to focus on as part of this preparation:

1. Skill Development: People with autism often have special skills or talents in areas like technology, art, math, or writing. Finding and encouraging these strengths can help

them get jobs. Joining training programs, workshops, or online classes can help them develop skills that match their interests.

2. Job Readiness Programs: Many organizations offer programs to help people with autism get ready for work. These programs teach how to write a resume, prepare for interviews, and improve communication skills. They provide a supportive space where individuals can practice what they need to succeed in a job.

3. Internships and Volunteer Opportunities: Gaining experience through internships or volunteering is a great way to learn about working and

build confidence. These opportunities allow individuals to try different jobs, learn new skills, and meet people who might help them find future employment.

4. Soft Skills Training: Employers want workers who can communicate well, work with others, and solve problems. Training programs that focus on these skills can help individuals with autism succeed in a job. Activities like role-playing and group exercises can improve these important skills.

5. Career Counseling: Talking to a career counselor can help individuals understand their strengths and explore different job options. A counselor can

help set realistic job goals and create a career plan that fits the person's unique needs and dreams.

Accommodations in the Workplace

To help individuals with autism do well at work, it's important to create a friendly and supportive work environment. Here are some common accommodations that can make a difference:

1. Flexible Work Arrangements: Allowing flexible hours or the option to work from home can help individuals balance their personal needs while still doing their job. This flexibility can help

reduce stress and improve how well they perform.

2. Structured Environment: Having a clear and organized work setting can help individuals feel more comfortable and focused. Clear job expectations, defined roles, and a regular routine can support their ability to complete tasks successfully.

3. Sensory-Friendly Workspaces: Some people with autism are sensitive to sounds and lights. Creating a workspace that minimizes distractions—like using quiet spaces or providing noise-canceling headphones—can help them feel more comfortable and productive.

4. Communication Supports: Using visual aids, written instructions, or simple language can help individuals understand their job tasks better. Clear communication and feedback can also reduce confusion.

5. Job Coaches or Mentors: Having a job coach or mentor can provide important support while working. They can offer training, help with workplace challenges, and encourage building good working relationships.

6. Regular Check-Ins: Meeting regularly with supervisors can help individuals stay on track, discuss any concerns, and receive helpful feedback. These meetings create open

communication and a supportive working relationship.

Encouraging Independence

Helping individuals with autism become more independent is essential as they grow up. Independence boosts self-esteem and allows individuals to take charge of their lives. Here are several strategies to encourage independence:

1. Life Skills Training: Teaching essential life skills—like managing money, cooking, and personal care—can help individuals lead more independent lives. Life skills programs

can provide chances to practice these skills in real situations.

2. Decision-Making Opportunities: Letting individuals make their own choices—big or small—can help them become more independent. This could be deciding what to wear, what to eat, or even what career they want to pursue. Encouraging them to make their own decisions builds confidence.

3. Goal Setting: Helping individuals set personal and job-related goals can provide motivation and direction. Breaking down big goals into smaller steps can make it easier and less overwhelming.

4. Social Skills Development: Encouraging social interactions can help individuals build friendships and support systems. Participating in social activities, clubs, or community groups can improve their social skills and provide opportunities to connect with others.

5. Encouraging Self-Advocacy: Teaching individuals to express their needs and preferences empowers them to take control of their lives. Self-advocacy includes communicating what they need, asking for help when necessary, and knowing their rights.

6. Promoting a Growth Mindset: Encouraging a positive mindset helps individuals understand that they can learn and improve from their experiences. Highlighting the importance of perseverance and resilience inspires them to overcome challenges and pursue their goals.

Getting individuals with autism ready for the workforce is an important step toward achieving independence and enhancing their overall quality of life. By focusing on skill development, providing necessary support at work, and promoting independence, families, educators, and employers can work together to create successful pathways to meaningful jobs. With the right preparation and support, individuals with autism can not only do well in their careers but also thrive as independent adults in society.

CHAPTER 13: ADVOCACY AND LEGAL RIGHTS

"The future belongs to those who believe in the beauty of their dreams."
– Eleanor Roosevelt

Advocacy is a strong way to help individuals with autism and their families. It helps them manage the challenges of life and secure their rights and protections. This chapter will explain what rights people with autism have, how to advocate for them, and how to help them speak up for themselves.

Understanding Rights and Protections

People with autism have certain rights and protections under various laws. Knowing these rights is crucial for getting the fair treatment and support they deserve. Here are some important laws that protect individuals with autism:

1. Americans with Disabilities Act (ADA): This law prevents discrimination against people with disabilities in areas like jobs, schools, and public services. It requires employers and schools to make adjustments so that individuals with autism can participate fully in society.

2. Individuals with Disabilities Education Act (IDEA): This law ensures that children with disabilities, including autism, receive a free and appropriate public education (FAPE). Schools must provide special education and services based on each child's unique needs. Each eligible student has an Individualized Education Program (IEP) that outlines specific learning goals and necessary support.

3. Section 504 of the Rehabilitation Act: This law prevents discrimination against people with disabilities in programs receiving federal funding, such as schools and colleges. Under Section 504, individuals with autism have the right to accommodations that

help them learn and participate in school activities.

4. Employment Protections: The ADA also provides protections for individuals with autism in the workplace. This means that employers cannot discriminate based on disability and must make reasonable adjustments to support workers with autism.

5. Health Care Rights: People with autism have the right to access health care and receive appropriate treatment. Laws like the Affordable Care Act (ACA) prohibit discrimination in health care coverage, ensuring that people get the services they need, including mental health care.

Advocating for Individuals with Autism

Advocacy means standing up for individuals with autism to help them get the support and services they need. Here are some effective ways to advocate for them:

1. Educate Others: Teaching people about autism and its characteristics can help reduce misunderstandings and promote empathy. Sharing personal experiences and information can create a more welcoming community.

2. Build a Support Network: Advocacy is often more effective when people work together. Connecting with other

families, autism organizations, and support groups creates a strong network that can work together for change.

3. Engage with Policymakers: Advocating for policy change is vital. Individuals and families can reach out to local, state, and federal lawmakers to promote laws that support people with autism. Writing letters, attending town meetings, and participating in advocacy events can make a difference.

4. Join Autism Organizations: Many organizations focus on advocating for individuals with autism. Being a part of these groups provides access to resources and opportunities to engage in advocacy. These organizations often

have connections with policymakers, making their efforts more effective.

5. Use Legal Resources: Families should know their legal rights and seek help when needed. Organizations specializing in disability rights can offer guidance and support in understanding and protecting these rights.

Promoting Self-Advocacy Skills

Self-advocacy means being able to express your needs, make decisions, and take control of your life. Teaching self-advocacy skills is essential for empowering individuals with autism. Here are some ways to promote these skills:

1. Encourage Communication: Helping individuals express their thoughts and feelings is vital for self-advocacy. This can involve practicing communication skills or using tools that assist with expression.

2. Provide Decision-Making Opportunities: Allowing individuals to make choices in their daily lives, like what to wear or eat, helps them gain confidence and a sense of control.

3. Set Goals: Teaching individuals to set personal goals helps them

understand their dreams and work toward achieving them. Breaking big goals into smaller steps can help track progress and celebrate successes.

4. Understand Rights: Educating individuals about their legal rights is important for effective self-advocacy. Knowing what rights they have can empower them to speak up for themselves and seek support when needed.

5. Practice Self-Advocacy Scenarios: Role-playing different situations can help individuals practice self-advocacy in a safe environment. This can include rehearsing conversations with teachers, employers, or doctors.

6. Encourage Self-Reflection: Encouraging individuals to think about their experiences helps them identify their strengths and areas for improvement, which builds ownership over their lives.

Advocacy and understanding legal rights are crucial for supporting individuals with autism. By learning about rights and protections, advocating for necessary support, and promoting self-advocacy skills, individuals with autism and their families can create a more inclusive and fair society. Advocacy helps individuals take control of their lives, access needed resources, and achieve their potential. By working together and promoting understanding, we can create a future where individuals with autism can thrive and contribute positively to their communities.

CHAPTER 14: THE INFLUENCE OF TECHNOLOGY

"Technology is best when it brings people together." - Matt Mullenweg

Technology is a big part of our everyday lives, and it can make a huge difference for people with autism. From tools that help them communicate to educational resources that make learning easier, technology can support and connect individuals with autism in meaningful ways. In this chapter, we will look at how technology affects the lives of those with autism by exploring assistive tools, online resources, and how technology can help with communication and learning.

Assistive Tools and Technology

Assistive technology includes devices and software that help people with disabilities do things they might find challenging. For individuals with autism, these tools can help with communication, social interactions, sensory processing, and daily tasks. Here are some important types of assistive tools and technologies that can benefit people with autism:

1. Communication Devices: Many people with autism have trouble

speaking. Augmentative and alternative communication (AAC) devices, like speech-generating tools and communication apps, can help them share their thoughts and needs. These devices let users pick pictures, symbols, or text, which the device then reads out loud, making communication easier.

2. Visual Supports: Visual aids like picture schedules, timers, and social stories help people understand what to expect in different situations. These tools can reduce anxiety and help them become more independent by providing clear visual information.

3. Sensory Tools: Many individuals with autism have strong sensitivities to sensory input. Tools like noise-canceling headphones, weighted blankets, and fidget toys can help them feel calm and manage sensory overload. Technology such as vibration devices or sensory apps can also provide soothing experiences.

4. Educational Software: There are many educational programs and apps designed for different learning styles. These tools can focus on social skills, emotional regulation, and academic subjects, providing tailored support that helps individuals with autism learn in a way that works for them.

5. Wearable Technology: Devices like smartwatches and fitness trackers can help individuals monitor their health and well-being. Some wearables can track stress levels, remind users to take breaks, or notify caregivers if help is needed.

Online Resources and Support Communities

The internet is full of helpful resources for individuals with autism, their families, and professionals. Online communities offer chances to connect, share information, and find support. Here are some key online resources and support communities:

1. Autism Organizations: Many organizations are dedicated to raising awareness about autism and supporting individuals and families. Websites like Autism Speaks, the Autism Society, and the National Autistic Society provide important information about autism and resources for those affected by it. These organizations often host webinars, newsletters, and events to connect people.

2. Support Groups: Online support groups and forums allow individuals and families to meet others who face similar challenges. These communities provide a safe place to share experiences, ask questions, and give advice. Social media platforms like Facebook and Reddit have various autism-related groups where people can find understanding and friendship.

3. Educational Resources: Websites like Khan Academy, ABCmouse, and various YouTube channels offer educational content for different age groups and learning styles. Many of these resources are free or low-cost, making learning more accessible for individuals with autism.

4. Parent and Caregiver Support: There are many websites that focus on helping parents and caregivers of individuals with autism. These sites provide articles, guides, and webinars on topics like behavior management, communication strategies, and self-care. Organizations like the Autism Society and TACA have special

sections for parents, offering tools and support for their journey.

5. Telehealth Services: Thanks to technology, telehealth services make it easier for people to find therapy, counseling, or educational support. Online platforms allow individuals to connect with therapists and specialists from their homes, which can be helpful for those who may have difficulty accessing services in person.

Utilizing Technology for Communication and Education

Technology can greatly improve communication and education for individuals with autism. By using various tools and platforms, they can learn to express themselves better and learn more effectively. Here are some ways to use technology for communication and education:

1. Communication Apps: Many apps are designed to help individuals with autism communicate. Apps like Proloquo2Go, TouchChat, and LAMP Words for Life let users communicate with symbols and text. These apps can be customized to fit each person's needs, making communication more personal.

2. Interactive Learning Tools: Technology can make learning more engaging and fun. Educational apps and games made for individuals with

autism can provide enjoyable ways to develop skills. These tools often use visual and auditory elements that cater to different learning styles.

3. Video Modeling: Video modeling is a helpful technique for teaching social skills and behaviors. By watching videos that show how to greet someone or follow directions, individuals can learn the desired behaviors. YouTube is a great platform for finding videos that model social situations.

4. Online Courses and Webinars: Many organizations offer online courses and webinars about autism. These opportunities allow individuals, families, and professionals to learn from experts and gain valuable

strategies for supporting individuals with autism.

5. Social Media for Connection: Social media can help individuals with autism connect with peers, share their experiences, and express themselves. By participating in online communities, they can form friendships, find support, and feel a sense of belonging.

6. Collaborative Tools: Technology also provides tools for teamwork, allowing individuals with autism to work together on projects or assignments. Platforms like Google Classroom, Microsoft Teams, and Zoom create opportunities for group learning and collaboration, helping

them improve social skills and work with others.

Technology has a powerful influence on the lives of individuals with autism. Assistive tools and online resources offer valuable support, making it easier for individuals to communicate, learn, and connect with others. By using technology, people with autism can become more independent, have better educational experiences, and build meaningful relationships. As technology continues to grow, it can open even more doors for individuals with autism, helping them thrive in their communities and reach their full potential.

CHAPTER 15: FUTURE DIRECTIONS IN AUTISM RESEARCH

"The future belongs to those who believe in the beauty of their dreams."
— Eleanor Roosevelt

As we learn more about autism, research in this field is moving forward quickly. Thanks to new technology and scientific discoveries, researchers are finding fresh insights into autism. This chapter will talk about what's happening right now in autism research, some new treatments that are being developed, and why including people with autism in the research process is so important.

Current Trends in Research

Autism research is making great progress, with scientists diving deep into various areas. Here are some key trends currently shaping autism research:

1. Genetics: Scientists are studying the genetic factors that contribute to autism. They're looking at how certain genes might be linked to autism to understand what causes it better. By

discovering these genetic links, researchers hope to create better tests and treatments tailored to each person.

2. Brain Imaging: New technologies like fMRI and DTI are helping scientists see what happens in the brains of people with autism. By examining how different parts of the brain connect and work together, researchers can learn more about the behaviors and challenges faced by those with autism, helping them design targeted therapies.

3. Early Detection: Detecting autism early can significantly improve outcomes for individuals. Researchers are working on ways to identify autism

sooner using behavioral tests and biological markers. When autism is diagnosed early, families can get help sooner, making interventions more effective.

4. Environmental Influences: Researchers are also exploring how environmental factors, like what a mother is exposed to during pregnancy, can affect the development of autism. Understanding these influences might help prevent autism in some cases.

5. Collaboration Across Fields: Since autism is complex, researchers from different areas—like psychology, neuroscience, and education—are coming together. This teamwork helps create a better understanding of autism and leads to more effective solutions.

New Therapeutic Innovations

As research progresses, new treatments are being developed to help individuals with autism. Here are some exciting innovations:

1. Behavioral Therapies: While Applied Behavior Analysis (ABA) is common, new methods like Acceptance and Commitment Therapy (ACT) are emerging. These approaches help individuals build emotional health and communication skills in more flexible ways.

2. Medication: There's no specific medication to cure autism, but

researchers are looking into drugs that can help manage symptoms, like anxiety and irritability. Some studies are focusing on medications that affect brain chemicals.

3. Technology: New therapies using virtual reality (VR) and augmented reality (AR) are being created to improve social skills and reduce anxiety. These technologies let individuals practice social situations in a safe environment.

4. Social Skills Programs: Innovative programs are being developed to teach important social skills to people with autism, often using engaging and

interactive methods that make learning fun.

5. Mindfulness Practices: More researchers are exploring how mindfulness and wellness techniques, such as yoga and relaxation strategies, can help reduce anxiety and improve emotional control in individuals with autism.

The Significance of Inclusive Research

Inclusive research means involving individuals with autism and their families in the research process. This is important for several reasons:

1. Empowerment: Including individuals with autism in research gives them a voice and empowers them. Their experiences can help shape research priorities and make sure studies are relevant to their lives.

2. Relevance: Research that includes the perspectives of people with autism is more likely to produce useful findings. By understanding what individuals with autism go through, researchers can develop better support strategies.

3. Reducing Stigma: Inclusive research challenges stereotypes about autism by highlighting the strengths and contributions of individuals with

autism. This can help change public perceptions and promote acceptance.

4. Encouraging Innovation: When people with autism share their insights, they can help researchers come up with new ideas and solutions. Their feedback can refine interventions and identify gaps in current services.

5. Creating Community: Involving individuals with autism in research builds a sense of community among researchers, individuals, and families. This teamwork can lead to a deeper understanding of autism and create resources to improve lives.

The future of autism research is exciting, with ongoing discoveries leading to better understanding and innovative treatments. It's crucial to prioritize inclusive research practices. By including individuals with autism and their families, we can ensure that research is meaningful and effective. Together, researchers and the autism community can create a brighter future where individuals with autism can thrive and reach their full potential.

CHAPTER 16: FOSTERING A SUPPORTIVE COMMUNITY

"Alone we can do so little; together we can do so much." – Helen Keller

Creating a supportive community for people with autism is very important for helping them grow and feel like they belong. As more people learn about autism, it's essential to create welcoming places that accept everyone's differences. In this chapter, we'll talk about how to make inclusive spaces, understand neurodiversity, and what everyone can do to help create a supportive community for individuals with autism.

Developing Inclusive Spaces

Inclusive spaces are places where people with autism can feel comfortable and succeed. These spaces are designed to meet different needs and make everyone feel welcome. Here are some ways to create inclusive spaces in various areas:

1. Schools: Schools are key in helping students with autism. Teachers can make classrooms inclusive by using different teaching methods to fit

various learning styles. Creating quiet areas where students can go if they feel overwhelmed is also helpful. Encouraging a culture of kindness and understanding among students can lead to friendships and support.

2. Community Centers and Recreation: Community centers should be friendly to all individuals, including those with autism. They can offer activities designed to include everyone and provide training for staff to understand the needs of individuals with autism. Sensory-friendly events like movie nights or art classes can give families enjoyable experiences.

3. Workplaces: Workplaces should be inclusive to help individuals with autism succeed. Employers can offer flexible work hours or remote options. Training coworkers on autism can create a supportive environment where everyone works together. Mentorship programs can also help individuals with autism navigate their jobs better.

4. Public Spaces: Parks and public areas should be designed to include everyone. These spaces can have quiet areas for relaxation and clear signs to help people find their way. Staff in these places should be trained to recognize and support individuals with autism to enhance everyone's experience.

Embracing Neurodiversity

Neurodiversity means understanding that everyone's brain works differently and that autism is just one of those variations. Accepting neurodiversity means recognizing that autism is a natural part of being human, not something that needs to be fixed. By embracing neurodiversity, we can create communities that value everyone's unique contributions.

1. Raising Awareness: Education is vital in embracing neurodiversity. Communities can hold workshops and events to teach people about autism and highlight the strengths of individuals with autism. Sharing success stories can help reduce myths and stigma.

2. Celebrating Talents: Many people with autism have special talents, whether in art, math, technology, or social skills. Communities can celebrate these talents by organizing events like talent shows or art exhibits that showcase individuals with autism.

3. Creating Support Networks: Support networks can help individuals with autism and their families feel connected. These networks can provide information, resources, and emotional support. Local support groups or online communities can help people share experiences and build friendships.

4. Advocating for Change: Advocacy is essential in promoting neurodiversity.

Communities can work together to create policies that support individuals with autism in education, jobs, and healthcare. This can lead to better resources and services for everyone.

How Everyone Can Participate

Building a supportive community for individuals with autism requires everyone's involvement—families, teachers, employers, and community members. Here are some ways you can help create a more inclusive environment:

1. Educate Yourself and Others: Learning about autism and sharing that

information with others can help create understanding and empathy. This can lead to more supportive interactions.

2. Volunteer: Many organizations support individuals with autism. Volunteering your time, whether at a local autism group or during events, can make a big difference in the lives of individuals and their families.

3. Be an Ally: Being an ally means standing up for individuals with autism and advocating for their rights. You can do this by speaking out against bullying and supporting inclusive activities.

4. Make Friends: Building friendships with individuals with autism can be rewarding. By reaching out and finding common interests, you can help them feel less alone. Simple gestures, like inviting someone to join an activity, can have a big impact.

5. Support Inclusive Initiatives: Get involved in or support programs that promote understanding and inclusion in your community. Attend workshops or events focused on autism to help raise awareness and show your support.

Creating a supportive community for individuals with autism takes teamwork and effort from everyone. By developing inclusive spaces, embracing neurodiversity, and encouraging participation from all community members, we can create environments where individuals with autism feel valued and empowered. Together, we can build a future that recognizes and celebrates the unique contributions of individuals with autism, helping everyone feel they belong.

Thank You Message

Dear Readers,

As we finish our journey through "AUTISM ESSENTIALS: Guidebook for Understanding and Managing Autism," I want to thank each of you. I'm so grateful that you chose this book and took the time to learn more about autism with kindness and respect.

Every person who learns about autism helps make the world a more accepting place. By understanding more, you're helping create a world that values and supports everyone, including those with autism.

I also want to say a special thank you to all the caregivers, teachers, and advocates who work so hard to help people with autism. This book is for you and all the amazing work you do.

Thank you again, and I hope what you've learned here continues to inspire you to be kind and supportive in everything you do. Please leave a positive review if this book has helped you.

With thanks,
David Greenwood

Made in the USA
Columbia, SC
24 January 2025